Trick or Treat
The History of Halloween

by Bill Uselton

Published by:
Southwest Radio Church
P.O. Box 1144 ● Oklahoma City, OK 73101
(800) 652-1144

Trick or Treat:
The History of Halloween

Halloween, the most horrifying of the ancient pagan holy days, is now upon us. While Christmas, Easter, and virtually all of the holidays have a pagan origin, the most obvious of these pagan holidays is Halloween. The ancient Babylonians would have recognized the pagan significance of the sunrise service, colored eggs, and bunny rabbits on Easter. The Romans would have recognized the large roasted bird, drunkenness, and gifts on Christmas. However, these two holidays have been greatly altered through history and are now cloaked in the religious superstition of our own time.

This is not true of All Hallows' Eve, more commonly known as Halloween, which is virtually identical today to the practices of those Druid-led worshippers in the Celtic lands of long ago. Very little difference exists between Halloween festivities now and Halloween festivities two thousand years ago. The reason ancient Halloween rites have not changed (unlike the ancient rites of December 25th) lies in the unique position of this ritual in terms of the occult.

The Roman Catholic Church has traditionally sought to dispose of pagan holidays by using the tried and true formula of accepting the local date and then merely changing the meaning and sometimes the ceremonies of the date. On Christmas these days, Santa Claus, gifts, and Christmas trees bear no resemblance whatsoever to the ancient December 25th practice of eviscerating a goose and using the internal organs to foretell the future, such as was the practice of the ancient, pagan Roman.

Ancient Celtic Roots

Altering holidays has met with much less success regarding Halloween, however, because this ancient Celtic ritual is more widely practiced now than ever before. Halloween is a practice that originated, as far as can be told, from the ancient Celtic peoples. The expanse of the Celtic race is related in Barry Cunliffe's book, *The Celtic World*:

> *"Traces of the Celts can be found almost anywhere in temperate Europe. Their fortifications—hill forts and oppida—are to be seen spreading in a broad arc from Yugoslavia to the north of Ireland; the museums of Europe store thousands of objects recovered from the excavations of graves and settlement sites or dredged from rivers and bogs; while many of our great cities, including Budapest, Paris, Belgrade, stand on Celtic foundations."*

Other famous cities are built on Celtic foundations: London, England, is a prime example. As to the identification of modern Celts, Ireland, Wales, and Scotland are populated largely by those of Celtic blood and retain the indigenous Celtic languages, as do the cities of Cornwall, England, and Brittany, France.

According to *Funk and Wagnall's Standard Reference Encyclo-*

---

pedia, Halloween, or "All Hallows' Eve" is:

> *". . . a name applied to the evening of October 31st, preceding the Christian fest of Hallowmass, Allhallows, or All Saint's Day. The observances connected with Halloween are believed to have originated among the ancient Druids, who believed that on that evening Saman, the lord of the dead, called forth hosts of evil spirits. The Druids customarily lit great fires on Halloween, apparently for the purpose of warding off these spirits. Among the ancient Celts, Halloween was the last evening of the year, and it was regarded as a propitious time for examining the portents of the future. The Celts also believed that the spirits of the dead revisited their earthly homes on that evening."*

Indications in our popular culture are that the public is becoming increasingly aware of the original rites of Halloween. Probably largely responsible for this reawakening are three movies which have grossed millions of dollars: *Halloween, Halloween II*, and *Halloween III—Season of the Witch*. In all three movies this cult of death, which is celebrated October 31st, is very well illustrated. Now, for the first time in possibly a thousand years, many know the origins and true significance of Halloween. Unfortunately, a marked rise in the ancient practices has accompanied this new knowledge. In England, Ireland, Scotland, France, and America, many thousands of persons are reverting to the religion of their ancestors and to the "festival of the dead."

Before examining modern witchcraft's rise in relation to Halloween and its affiliated rituals, we should consult the Bible. Exodus 22:18 says, *"Thou shalt not suffer a witch to live."* The Bible contains repeated denunciations of witchcraft and other practices of this ilk. Therefore, claims by modern witches that they are not "opposed" to Christianity are contradicted by the Scriptures.

Exodus 22:20 further warns, *"He that sacrificeth unto any god, save unto the LORD only, he shall be utterly destroyed."* Thus, although the numbers of those who practice the black arts are growing, we must remember that the ancient practices of sacrifice and witchcraft are expressly forbidden.

Man, Myth, and Magic, a twenty-four–volume encyclopedia of the supernatural, says:

> *"All Hallows' Eve, or Hallowe'en, was originally a festival of fire and the dead and the powers of darkness. It is the evening of 31 October, the night before the Christian festival of All Hallows' or All Saint's Day. All Hallows' Day commemorates the saints and martyrs, and was first introduced in the seventh century. Its date was changed from 13 May to 1 November in the following century, probably to make it coincide with and Christianize a pagan festival of the dead. All Soul's Day in the Roman Catholic calendar is 2 November. It is marked by prayers for the souls of the dead."*

While the Roman Catholic Church enjoyed success in converting the originally pagan holidays of Christmas and Easter to more "Christianized" counterparts, this was not the case with Halloween. The intentional effort by the Catholic Church to stamp out the pagan ceremonies of Halloween failed. There are those who would state that the modern-day ritual practice of Halloween is harmless fun for children and adults alike. Dressing up in costumes, going for "trick-or-treat," creating large bonfires, and using pumpkins to create "jack-o'-lanterns" are all part of a harmless charade perpetrated once a year. While the original meanings of these rituals may have been lost or clouded in the minds of most people today, the actual methodology of witchcraft and worship survives to the present day. Therefore, it would seem prudent for any concerned Christian to examine the original meanings of the modern-day rituals associated with Halloween.

Demons, Hobgoblins, and Witches

Let us specifically examine the original meanings of Halloween. *The Golden Bough*, by Sir James Frazier, is a considered and respected, albeit secular, work on the occult from the nineteenth century. Sir Frazier's comments seem most enlightening to our study.

> *"Throughout Europe, Halloween, the night which marks the transition from autumn to winter, seems to have been of old the time of year when the souls of the departed were supposed to revisit their old homes in order to warm themselves by the fire and to comfort themselves with the good cheer provided for them in the kitchen or the parlour by their affectionate kinsfolk. It was, perhaps, a natural thought that the approach of winter should drive the poor shivering ghosts from the bare fields and the leafless woodlands to the shelter of the cottage with its familiar fireside."*

Thus, one of the original reasons for bonfires so prevalent during Halloween was to attract the dead and to keep them away from the home, until their journey into the afterworld was complete. This was a serious matter to those who practiced the Celtic religion. Samhain, or Sa-ween as it was pronounced, hence Halloween, was the single most important festival concerning the dead to the ancient Celtic world.

Bonfires were also used for one of the most hideous acts imaginable. The *Lacrousse Encyclopedia of Mythology* tells us: *"On the eve of Samain the people of the side* [otherworld] *left their domain and wandered in the world of man. . . . Attacks by hostile supernatural powers and of sacrifices are indicative of this insecurity and the need for propitiation."*

Simply put, the Celts wished to know the future and believed that on this terrible night they could learn the future by the use of a ritual. This ritual consisted of constructing a basket containing a human being or an animal. This basket was then burned with the unfortunate inmate within burned to death. It was the belief of the Celts that by watching the victim die by fire, they would be able to see signs of the future as the sacrificial victim passed from this world into the next.

Foretelling the future was an idea the Celts found intriguing. The Catholics correctly compared the Celtic Druids to the witches because of their pagan practice of using bonfires to predict the future. However, the practice of burning sacrificial animals, and occasionally people, remained unabated for many centuries despite Catholic attempts to "Christianize" the holiday. Even in our time, animals are sacrificed on Halloween in Europe and in the Philippines, as well as in the Americas. It is also interesting to note that in some large American cities, the problem of arson during Halloween has become increasingly widespread. Some large cities have reported as many as two hundred arson fires set to houses (both vacant and occupied), warehouses, churches, and office buildings during a typical Halloween night.

While most modern-day Halloween bonfires (hopefully!) are not to sacrifice humans, its original meaning alludes to a time when such a heinous ritual was used for the vilest intentions. The Bible is quite clear in denouncing such a horrendous practice. The Lord condemned King Ahaz because he burned his children in the fire to the pagan Gentile gods (2 Kings 16:3; 2 Chron. 28:3). Such an act brought shame and defeat to King Ahaz, as he was later conquered

Genjie's

by both the Assyrians and his brethren of the northern kingdom of Israel.

The Celts believed that on this night other creatures roamed with the spirits of the dead. Fairies, as reported by *Man, Myth, and Magic*, ". . . could also be seen on All Hallows' Eve, moving from one fairy hill to another with the music of bells and elfhorns. They were sometimes identified with the dead."

The Celts held that fairies could be good or bad; however, the introduction of Christianity changed this distinction. Jack Santino's work, *Night of the Wandering Souls*, reveals:

> "Samhain, with its emphasis on the supernatural, was very pagan. While missionaries identified Christian holy days with native holy days, they branded the earlier supernatural deities as evil and associated them with the Devil. As representatives of the rival religion, Druids were considered evil; their gods and spirits, devilish and demonic. The Celtic underworld inevitably became associated with the Christian Hell. The effects of this policy were to diminish but not totally dispel beliefs in the traditional gods. According to priests, fairies were fallen angels, thus identifying them with devils in Christian theology."

Thus, as the Celts converted to the new religion, they did not forget their stories of the dead traveling to the afterworld on Halloween, nor did sightings and activities of fairies cease being reported. Instead, manifestations of this night became overwhelmingly evil, and the festival adopted even more malicious overtones. Everything supernatural was attributed to demons who masqueraded as fairies, hobgoblins, vampires, werewolves, and virtually any other myth. Interestingly, until the advent of the twentieth century, these supernatural beings were regarded as very real and very dangerous.

As more Celts became Christian, the native Druids or Celtic priests were correctly labeled "witches." Witch-hunting became a very common phenomenon until the seventeenth century, with the usual punishment prescribed being burning at the stake. Whereas witch-hunting crazes broke out indiscriminately, hunting witches during Halloween became virtually a national pastime. *Man, Myth, and Magic* says:

> "*Darker and colder creatures still roamed through the night on Hallowe'en—demons and hobgoblins, witches who straddled broomsticks or shankbones, flew in sieves or eggshells, or rode on coal-black horses. The fires helped to keep them off and at Balmoral in Queen Victoria's time the effigy of a hideous old witch was ceremoniously burned on a bonfire at Hallowe'en.*"

White Magic

It should be noted that Queen Victoria ruled the British Empire at its height, during the nineteenth century. Witches were very much on the public's mind during the last two millennia. Midnight of October 31st was considered to be an extremely hazardous time, as witches were believed to be actively hexing people and communing with the Devil. Many Catholics took to making charms and casting "white magic" spells to protect themselves from the evil they knew to be very potent on this night. What many apparently did not realize was that the charms themselves were as evil as the witches they were supposed to thwart.

Many people still believed the Druids could foretell the future. As the Catholics believed the Druids were witches—or in the case of males, warlocks—they did not doubt this.

Using witchcraft to foretell the future was a crime that cost King Saul of Israel his life. First Samuel 28:7–8 reads, *"Then said Saul unto his servants, Seek me a woman that hath a familiar spirit, that I may go to her, and enquire of her. And his servants said to him, Behold, there is a woman that hath a familiar spirit at En-dor. And Saul disguised himself, and put on other raiment, and he went, and two men with him, and they came to the woman by night: and he said, I pray thee, divine unto me by the familiar spirit, and bring me him up, whom I shall name unto thee."*

The story of the witch of Endor possessed several significant similarities to the witches of the Celts. Familiar spirits are nothing more than demons, and the fairies and leprechauns of Celtic myths are the same as familiar spirits.

The Lord's punishment upon Saul was pronounced to him the very same night. First Samuel 28:17–18 relates, *"And the LORD hath done to him, as he spake by me: for the LORD hath rent the kingdom out of thine hand, and given it to thy neighbour, even to David: Because thou obeyedst not the voice of the LORD, nor executedst his fierce wrath upon Amalek, therefore hath the Lord done this thing unto thee this day."* The Lord's pronouncements concerning witchcraft are quite clear. There is no such thing as "white" magic; it is all evil and empowered by evil beings. It should also be emphasized that these actions transpired at nighttime, as do traditional Halloween activities.

The other, and much more popular, so-called "white" magic act is the creation and wearing of charms. Few people realize that the wearing and use of charms is simply another manifestation of witchcraft. Be it rabbits' feet, religious medallions, trinkets, or other such relics, these objects are subject to demonic power. The word *charm* means "to cast a spell on."

The Bible contains several passages about charms and the use thereof. Psalm 58:3–5 says, *"The wicked are estranged from the womb: they go astray as soon as they be born, speaking lies. Their poison is like the poison of a serpent: they are like the deaf adder that stoppeth her ear; Which will not hearken to the voice of charmers, charming never so wisely."* This is hardly a ringing endorsement for the use of charms.

Furthermore, Isaiah 19:3 states, *"And the spirit of Egypt shall fail in the midst thereof; and I will destroy the counsel thereof: and they shall seek to the idols, and to the charmers, and to them that have familiar spirits, and to the wizards."* The Lord purposefully groups together idol worshippers, witches with familiar spirits, wizards, and charmers. This is not the only scripture dealing thusly.

The activities of Halloween, the making of charms, divining the future, the practice of magic, and dealing with unclean spirits and demons are expressly forbidden to mankind. Deuteronomy 18:10–12 says, *"There shall not be found among you any one that maketh his son or his daughter to pass through the fire, or that useth divination, or an observer of times, or an enchanter, or a witch, Or a charmer, or a consulter with familiar spirits, or a wizard, or a necromancer* [that is, "one who seeks to interrogate the dead," according to Scofield]. *For all that do these things are an abomination unto the LORD: and because of these abominations the LORD thy God doth drive them out from before thee."* This is a very explicit commandment from the Lord. Thus, the ancient Celtic ritual of Halloween practiced today in America is pagan in origin and innately linked with the occult, about which the Bible has much to say.

Trick-or-Treat

Another modern-day Halloween ritual is "trick-or-treat," where children dress up in costumes and roam from house to house asking for food and candy. Presumably, if the inquiry for food and candy is refused, a trick to the homeowner results. This practice, which became quite prevalent during this century, has increasingly fallen into disfavor by many parents of small children. During the 1970s and 1980s, incidents of small children receiving poisoned candy and cookies, and apples concealing razor blades and fish hooks, have made many parents fearful to take their children on the traditional neighborhood trick-or-treat routes. In recent years, even hospitals have offered to voluntarily x-ray candy to determine if tampering has taken place. Increasingly, parents have started taking their children to prearranged trick-or-treats at shopping malls where merchants hand out candy from the store fronts. While this practice should help ensure that the practice of trick-or-treat is safer, this does not change the fact that trick-or-treat has pagan and occult origins in the first place.

Among the Celts—as well as among the Chinese, the Egyptians, and even the Aztecs—it was thought that the spirits of the dead required food and drink. During the festival of Samhain, the people would leave various articles of food outside to placate the spirits. This was very important, for only the finest mutton legs, vegetables, eggs, and poultry—as well as honey and wine—were left outside for the spirits to consume on their way to the netherworld. To supply nothing meant that the hungry and possibly irritated spirit might intrude upon one's house and help itself to one's belongings. Leaving out food that had spoiled was also considered an open invitation to disaster. Therefore, families who faced uncertain diets, often of very low quality, gave what was most precious to them: food. This takes on added implications when we recall that, at that time, food was very difficult to preserve. Moreover, Halloween marked winter's beginning, when food was at its scarcest, and starvation was not uncommon.

From this practice evolved one of the most remarkable aspects of Halloween; to quote Santino:

"Virtually all of our Halloween customs today can be traced to the ancient Celtic day of the dead. Each of Halloween's many mysterious customs has a history, or at least a story, behind it. The wearing of costumes, for instance, and the roaming from door to door demanding treats can be traced to the Celtic period and the first few centuries of Christianity when it was thought that the souls of the dead were out and around, along with fairies, witches, and demons. Food and drink were left out to placate them. As the centuries wore on, people began dressing as these dreadful creatures and performing antics in exchange for offerings of food and drink. This practice, called mumming, evolved into our present trick-or-treating. To this day, witches, ghosts, and skeleton figures of the dead are among the favorite disguises."

The practice of wearing masks and outfits to represent these evil creatures is universal in the human experience. From the Indians of America to China—in all the inhabited areas of the earth—traditions exist in which individuals who dress to represent a god or demon are embued with supernatural powers and often given presents or beneficial treatment. There is a reason for this. Idols and masks of idols are *representative* of something! First Corinthians 10:19–21 says, *"What say I then? that the idol is any thing, or that which is offered in sacrifice to idols is any thing? But I say, that the things which the Gentiles sacrifice, they sacrifice to devils, and not to God: and I would not that ye should have fellowship with devils. Ye cannot drink the cup of the Lord, and the cup of devils: ye cannot be partakers of the Lord's table, and of the table of devils."* So the Bible tells us that idols represent demons, *demon* being the actual word used in the original Greek text. Offerings of food are offerings of food to demons; the trick-or-treating of today is reminiscent of that practice. In fact, trick-or-treating children often masquerade as demons. Food is given these children under this guise of a "trick or a treat." It has become a recent phenomenon that adults participate in these activities, a strange shadow of what transpired two thousand years earlier.

Lest we should become confused as to how the concept of romping spirits became intertwined with children, we must again quote *Man, Myth, and Magic*:

> *"The guisers went from house to house, singing and dancing. Their blood-curdling masks and grotesque costumes may have been meant to keep evil at bay, or, more likely, were a visible representation of the ghosts and goblins that lurked in the night. The masks have now been transferred to the children who, in the United States, visit the neighbours for the food offerings which belonged to the dead—or play tricks akin to the legendary destructiveness of witches and imps abroad on this night."*

This is the story and significance behind trick-or-treating. But there is more to the story of Halloween . . .

The Jack-O'-Lantern

Virtually everyone in this country has either made or seen a jack-o'-lantern. These macabre, grinning pumpkins with candles inside often light the way of the errant ghost seeking his or her candy. Have you ever wondered where the idea for the jack-o'-lantern originated? This, too, was a Celtic invention used during the ritual of Samhain or Halloween. In the United States, the jack-o'-lantern is a carved pumpkin. The orange, grinning, candle-filled lamp of Halloween is extremely popular and may be observed virtually anywhere in the United States on Halloween. The use of a pumpkin for the jack-o'-lantern is an invention of the American Indian. In Europe, where the concept for the jack-o'-lantern was conceived, it is not a pumpkin but rather a carved-out turnip. The switch was made in America because, besides being much larger than the turnip, the pumpkin is easier to carve. The turnip was the original jack-o'-lantern, and here is the earliest known tale of how it originated.

The tale of the jack-o'-lantern is, in several ways, reminiscent of the classic tale of Dr. Faustus in world literature. A blacksmith by the name of Jack made a contract with Satan. The deal contained a trade-off. Jack the blacksmith would be given powers by Satan that would make him the best blacksmith in the world for a period of seven years. In return, Satan would demand Jack's soul

---

at the end of this seven-year period. Jack thus received the powers and hung a sign outside his shop proclaiming himself the master of all masters.

As the story goes, one day the Son of God came to the shop, accompanied by the apostle Peter. The sign had indicated that the owner was in need of religious indoctrination. Thus, the two worked several miracles—to no avail—in Jack's presence. Peter then offered Jack three wishes, which Jack immediately seized upon. Santino writes:

> *"First, he wished that whenever he told someone to climb a nearby pear tree that person would have to stay in the tree until Jack allowed him to come down. He made the same wishes regarding his armchair and his purse: one must stay in them until Jack allowed him to go. 'You have wished very foolishly,' said Saint Peter. 'You should have wished for everlasting peace in Heaven.' Nevertheless, Jack used these three wishes to trick the Devil when he came to take his soul. Each time the Devil came, Jack tricked him into climbing the tree, sitting in his chair, and finally, shrinking himself and entering his purse. Each time, the Devil gave Jack seven years in return for his freedom, and finally he simply fled in terror."*

Jack could not live forever, however, and one day he died. When presented at Heaven's pearly gates, Peter would not allow Jack inside. Denied entrance into Heaven, Jack went to Hell. At the gates of Hell, Satan refused Jack entrance, saying that Jack was full of too many tricks and would cause mischief. Satan then ordered the gates of Hell closed. But before Jack was thrown out, he managed to scoop out a burning coal from the fires of Hell with a turnip he had been eating. As this coal came from Hell, it was eternal and would never be extinguished. Thus, Jack, who was denied entrance into Heaven and Hell, was doomed to roam the earth with his peculiar lantern, his jack-o'-lantern, if you will.

Halloween Today

The Halloween festival became fully established in America after the huge influx of Irishmen as a result of the great Irish potato famine of 1846. America, in that era, was quite religious, and so the stories of fairies and leprechauns, as well as demons and ghosts, were accepted as fact. Religious beliefs aside, those less well-educated tend to be more superstitious—at least that was the prevalent thinking of the early to mid-twentieth century. In America, those who were the most superstitious were also the least-educated; the American Indian, the Negro, and the poor, white settlers in the Appalachian and Ozark regions tended to take superstitions very seriously indeed. Other than these groups, belief in the Bible as the Word of God confirmed, as a matter of course, the existence of ghosts and demons. Education—as taught in the mid-twentieth century until the present—has become increasingly secular and anti-supernatural in thinking.

Generally, we tend to think the more educated secular population in society is less superstitious. However, with the rise of the New Age movement, an increase in the practice of so-called "natural religions" or paganism has occurred. A great many of the adherents to modern New Age philosophy are professional, well educated individuals. This has also resulted in an increased interest in the occult, and the high holiday of the occult, Halloween.

This is not merely a history lesson, but is a warning. The study of the history of Halloween is necessary for all concerned Christians, for the practice of observing Halloween honors a force that is as real today as it was two thousand years ago. We like to believe when the apostolic gifts diminished in the first century that the opposition of demonic influence and possession died out as well. However, nothing could be further from the truth. Demonic influence and possession afflict this country now as never before. Studies in the occult, from both religious and purely academic points of view, have shown a marked increase in the numbers and efforts of Satanists in the latter part of this century. By Satanists we include such practices as witchcraft, following pagan religions, charmers, necromancers, and other practices of the black arts.

According to Paul Lee Tan's *Encyclopedia of 7700 Illustrations*:

> *"Satan worship and all forms of the occult are evident everywhere. It is estimated that there are at least 100 million Americans who dabble in some form of black magic. In New Jersey, a young man was drowned by a group of his friends at his request, because he believed that a violent end would put him in command of forty legions of demons."*

Witchcraft is not dead. In England, at the ancient ruins of Stonehenge, Druid priests perform ancient rites as their ancestors did. Witch hunts, which resulted in the murdering of more than half a million persons in Europe during the last millennia, are not a phenomenon of the past. According to *Collier's Encyclopedia*: *"In 1957 during a virus epidemic in Alaska, the civil authorities were hard put to prevent an Eskimo community from destroying the 'witches' held responsible."*

No, the occult is not dead. In fact, the occult is currently probably stronger than at any time since the Dark Ages. Zombies are no laughing matter in Haiti, any more than demons are to Christians; and who is to say in what form demonic power can manifest itself? Astrology, chiefest of the black arts among Americans, has skyrocketed in popularity since the 1960s. According to the *Ency-*

clopedia of 7700 Illustrations:

> *"Americans spend over $200 million a year on astrology alone. A 1976 Gallup poll indicated that those who take astrology seriously may number as many as 32 million. . . . It is estimated that twelve hundred of the seventeen hundred U.S. daily newspapers regularly print horoscope columns."*

Even the American Indian tribes, some of which were intense occultists, never had the social problems we have today. The August 6, 1991, edition of *The Daily Oklahoman*, printed an extremely pertinent article by Thomas Sowell. Mr. Sowell, a black conservative, is recognized as one of the most articulate critics of Marxist liberalism. In his article entitled "'Experts' Are Endangering Society," he used the recent serial killings committed by Jeffrey Dahmer to illustrate the shortcomings of our liberal society. In the article, he recognized the price for our society's rejection of the laws of God:

> *"Has anyone asked just whose bright idea it was to parole the man who has now confessed to multiple murders in Milwaukee? Of course not. Whoever it was does not even suffer the penalty of public embarrassment. All across this country, shrinks, 'experts,' can recommend the early release of the most vicious and dangerous criminals, without being the least bit accountable for the consequences."*

Many people in this country are deeply involved in evil for evil's sake. The serial killer Richard Ramirez, known as "The Night Stalker," yelled "Hail, Satan!" at his trial. Recently, Jeffrey Dahmer's homosexual murders shocked the nation. A woman he briefly dated stated that she saw the candles flicker out when Jeffrey Dahmer said in a seance, "Let's contact Lucifer." Fortunately, she had the good sense to leave. Finally, the words of Edward Gein directly implicate the reality of evil as a force. Serial killer Edward Gein was a reclusive bachelor who committed such heinous crimes as grave robbing, fratricide, mutilation, murder, and even cannibalism in the small Wisconsin town of Plainfield in the late 1950s. Mr. Gein was the source material for the "Norman Bates" character in the movie *Psycho*, as well as for the character of "Leatherface" in the movie *Texas Chainsaw Massacre*. Harold Schechter's book, *Deviant: The Shocking True Story of Ed Gein, the Original Psycho*, states:

> *"Eddie, too, as it turned out, felt that he was driven to his ghoulish activities by an irresistible force which he experienced and described to his interrogators as an 'evil spirit' invading his mind from someplace outside himself."*

The Cal Thomas editorial titled "Goodness v. Evil: Spiritual Explanation for Mass Murder," in the August 6, 1991, edition of *The Daily Oklahoman*, sheds some additional light on this subject:

> *"People in Milwaukee, like those in Houston eighteen summers ago* [the Dean Coryll murders], *wonder why the police or neighbors or someone did not notice what went on in these houses or the disappearance of so many people. An explanation is that our culture still believes that people are basically good and so tries to ignore things that do not conform to that presumption.* [Dr. M. Scott] *Peck says he has been asked dozens of times why evil exists, 'yet no one ever asked me, . . . "Why is there good in the world?" It is as if we automatically assume this is a naturally good world that has somehow been contaminated by evil.' The opposite is not only more plausible, but the evidence seems to support such a conclusion that man is basically not good and needs to be controlled and confronted to a common standard of goodness."*

Something is wrong, all right. The earth was good until Adam fell and all men fell with him. Man's fallen nature and the curse on the earth are being felt even now. How dangerous it is to act as if evil is not a force!

The evil world of the occult wages an ongoing assault against Christianity. We believe revival of witchcraft and the black arts is indicative of the end times. Satan knows the time of Christ's return is near, and he is mustering all of his forces to engage in a battle he has lost already. Let no one doubt that witchcraft and sorcery are very real. The number of occult-related murders has been on the increase in this country for more than a generation. Moreover, one of the most significant occult dates of all—the one favored for the Black Mass—is Halloween, celebrated the last day of October in our nation. On college campuses and universities today, Anton LaVey's *Satanic Bible* is often a bestseller—in some cases, outselling the Bible itself.

It is of great importance to realize that the powers some claim are not powers of themselves: real sorcery relies on demonic or satanic power. Ephesians 6:12 states, *"For we wrestle not against flesh and blood, but against principalities, against powers, against the rulers of the darkness of this world, against spiritual wickedness in high places."* There is, in conclusion, only one way to win against Satan; that is victory through Christ Jesus.

HALLOWEEN—
the most horrifying of the ancient pagan holy days

While Christmas, Easter, and virtually all of the holidays have a pagan origin, the most obvious of these pagan holidays is Halloween. "All Hallows' Eve," or "Hallowe'en," was originally a festival of fire and the dead and the powers of darkness.

This is not merely a history lesson, but is a warning. The study of the history of Halloween is necessary for all concerned Christians, for the practice of observing Halloween honors a force that is as real today as it was 2,000 years ago.

ISBN 1-879366-89-4   B-831